THE SKY IS AWAKE!

THE CONSTELLATIONS

Astronomy for Beginners

Children's Astronomy & Space Books

BABY PROFESSOR
EDUCATION KIDS

Speedy Publishing LLC

40 E. Main St. #1156

Newark, DE 19711

www.speedypublishing.com

Copyright 2017

In this book, we're going to talk about the constellations in the night sky. So, let's get right to it!

WHAT IS A CONSTELLATION?

A constellation is composed of stars. The stars may be millions of light years away from each other, but in the night sky they form a pattern when they are observed from Earth.

Orion Nebula

The pattern might look something like a person or it might look like an animal or other object. Some of the stars in a constellation might look a lot brighter than others. Most of the constellations don't look much if anything like the objects they are supposed to be.

WHY DID ANCIENT PEOPLE USE THE CONSTELLATIONS?

Our ancient ancestors knew the skies very well. They used the constellations as a way to keep track of time throughout the year so they knew the right time to plant their crops and when to harvest them. They also used them like a map for navigation.

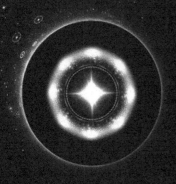

By locating the constellation of Ursa Minor in the night sky, they were able to locate Polaris, which is the North Star. By using the North Star's height in the sky, ship navigators could pinpoint their latitude as they traveled across the vast oceans.

In addition to these practical purposes, the constellations also had a spiritual purpose. These patterns reminded them of the stories of their mythology, which was a form of religion at that time. The constellations also gave ancient peoples a sense of their position in the vast expanse of the universe.

Ptolemy

HOW MANY CONSTELLATIONS ARE THERE?

In the year 150 AD, the Greek astronomer Ptolemy published a book called The Almagest. He summarized a great deal of the astronomical knowledge that the ancient Greeks had in this book. His book was a list of over 1,000 stars. Ptolemy estimated the brightness of the stars. He also listed 48 constellations.

His listing was the foundation of our modern system of constellations. These constellations had ties to Greek mythology. Other cultures like the Babylonians and Egyptians had mythologies attached to their constellations as well. Different cultures saw different patterns in the stars.

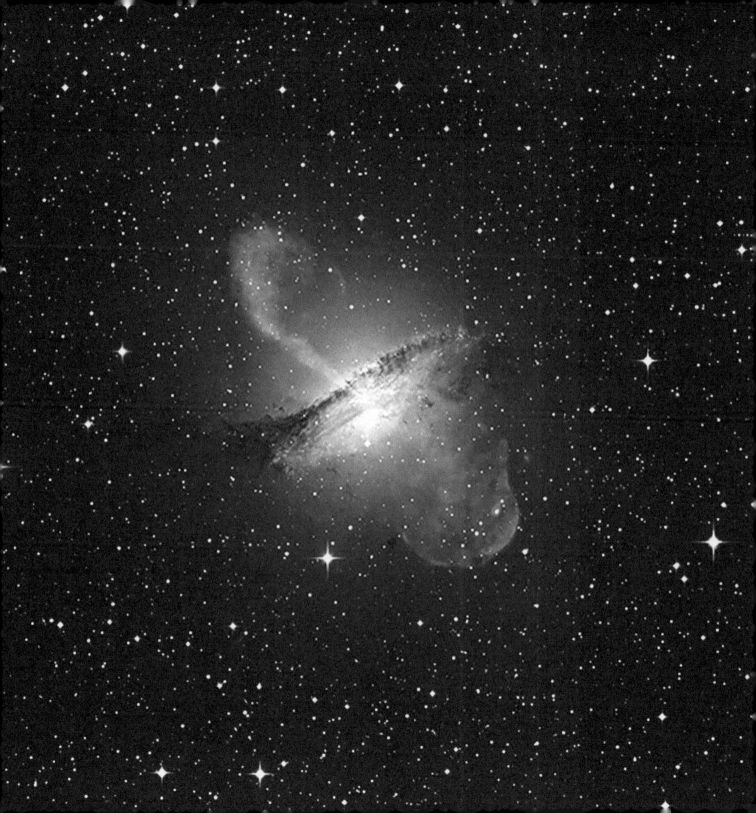

The International Astronomical Union, IAU for short, had its first official meeting in 1922. They are the organization responsible for the names of celestial bodies.

At their meeting, they officially sanctioned the 88 constellations that we use today. With these additions to Ptolemy's list, stars, nebulas, and galaxies, no matter how faint they are to the naked eye, fall somewhere within a constellation. For today's working astronomers, constellations are more a way to divide up the night sky than a way to see patterns in it.

THE NORTHERN AND SOUTHERN HEMISPHERE

Depending on where you are observing on Earth, you may not be able to see all the constellations. Constellation maps are organized by the northern and southern hemispheres. The seasons you are viewing the night sky will make a difference in which constellations you see as well.

WHY DO THE CONSTELLATIONS SEEM TO MOVE IN THE SKY?

The constellations appear to move very slowly during the course of the night. They rotate around the North Star. If you look at a constellation as soon as it gets dark, and then you view it a few hours later, you'll be able to observe its "movement." The important thing to remember is that the constellations aren't really moving at all. It's the movement of the Earth as it rotates on its axis that causes this illusion.

Constellations

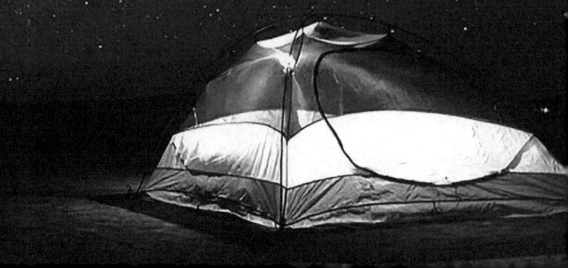

WILL THE CONSTELLATIONS ALWAYS LOOK THE SAME?

The patterns of the constellations that we see in the sky today don't look that different than they did thousands of years ago. We know this because there are many written records.

However, the stars that we see in the sky are all moving very fast away from our Sun. The reason we don't perceive this is because they are so far away from us. It will take thousands of lifetimes for the patterns to be visibly different than they are today.

Stars

Telescope

USING A STAR MAP

To find the constellations, all you need is a good star map and either binoculars or a telescope. There are printed maps, but you can also get a star map that's customized to your location and time of year if you use a software application.

You'll be able to make out the outlines of the constellations with the naked eye, but with binoculars or a telescope you'll be able to see the stars that are fainter. You'll also be able to make out nebulae as well as star clusters. The darker the sky is, the better your visibility will be.

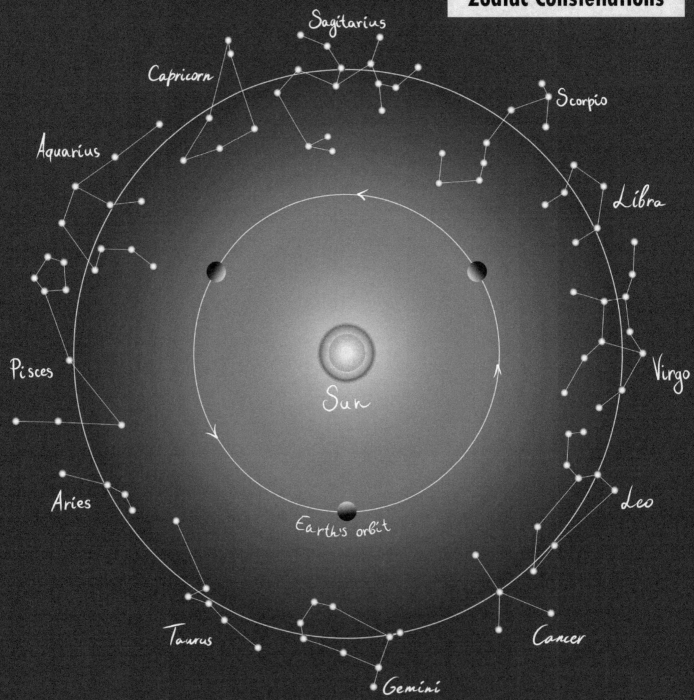

Zodiac Constellations

WHAT IS THE ZODIAC?

The zodiac constellations are a specific group of 13 constellations. They are located in a special band in the sky that is about 23 degrees in width. This is the location where the Sun, the planets, and our moon appear to be traveling. In ancient times and still today, these constellations are used to predict horoscopes in astrology, which is a spiritual practice, not a science.

The 12 constellations used
as astrological signs are:

- ⮎ **Aquarius, from January 20 to February 18**
- ⮎ **Pisces, from February 19 to March 20**
- ⮎ **Aries, from March 21 to April 19**
- ⮎ **Taurus, from April 20 to May 20**
- ⮎ **Gemini, from May 21 to June 20**
- ⮎ **Cancer, from June 21 to July 22**
- ⮎ **Leo, from July 23 to August 22**
- ⮎ **Virgo, from August 23 to September 22**
- ⮎ **Libra, from September 23 to October 22**
- ⮎ **Scorpius for the sign of Scorpio, from October 23 to November 21**
- ⮎ **Sagittarius, from November 22 to December 21**
- ⮎ **Capricornus for the sign of Capricorn, from December 22 to January 19**

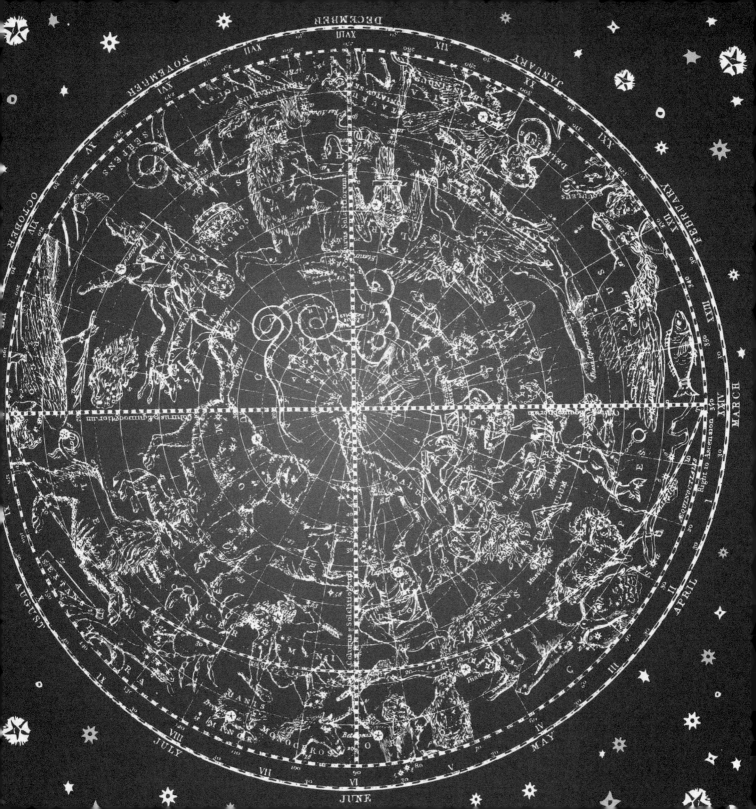

FAMOUS CONSTELLATIONS THAT ARE VISIBLE IN THE NORTHERN HEMISPHERE

Although their best viewing month is listed, many of these constellations can be seen in the Northern Hemisphere for 6 months or more.

AQUARIUS

This zodiac constellation is best seen in October. It's large, but it's also faint, which makes it difficult to locate. In Greek stories, Zeus, the king of the gods invited a handsome youth by the name of Ganymede to become the cup bearer to the gods on Mount Olympus.

Aquarius

Aquarius means "carrier of the cups." Ganymede stayed forever young and he was given a famous position in the night sky for eternity. The line of stars on the right of this constellation represent Ganymede's right arm. You'll definitely need a dark sky outside the city limits to identify this constellation.

AQUILA

This constellation is best seen in late summer or early September. In Greek mythology, Aquila is the eagle that kidnapped Ganymede and brought him to his new home at Mount Olympus. The eagle also carried the thunderbolts that Zeus sometimes threw in the sky. This pattern of stars is located in the band of the Milky Way. Its brightest star is Altair.

Aquila

ARIES

ARIES

This zodiac constellation is best seen in December. Aries represents a ram and in Greek mythology, it's the ram whose fleece was the Golden Fleece in the ancient story of Jason of the Argonauts. Jason must get the fleece to become king. The orange giant star called Hamal is the brightest star in Aries.

CANIS MAJOR

This constellation is best seen in February and its name means the "greater dog." It represents Orion's hunting dog called Laelaps. He trails behind the hunter Orion as Orion sets out to hunt Taurus the bull. Laelaps was able to race so fast that Zeus gave him a position in the skies for eternity. This constellation contains the star called Sirius, which is the brightest star seen from Earth.

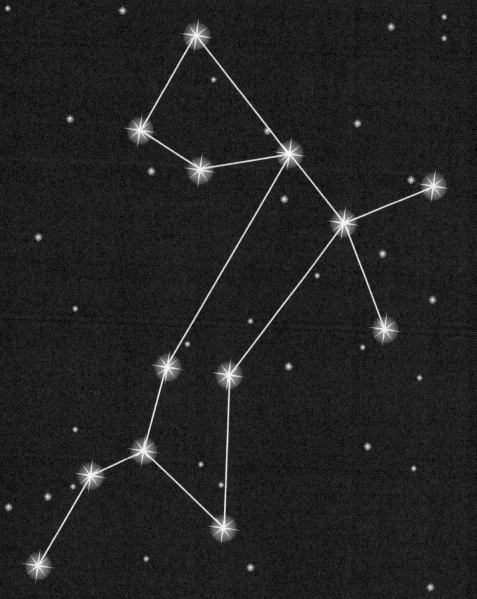

Canis Major

CASSIOPEIA

This constellation is best seen in November and is named after a boastful queen. Cassiopeia thought she was more beautiful than the sea nymphs were, so she was banished to the sky forever. This constellation has a clear "W" shape so it's easy to recognize.

This constellation is best seen in January and is one of the easiest constellations to recognize. Due to its position in the sky, it can be seen throughout the world. Orion in Greek mythology was an enormous hunter, who was Poseidon's son. He hunted side by side with the goddess Artemis. Different myths say that he was killed by her or the sting of Scorpius, the scorpion. 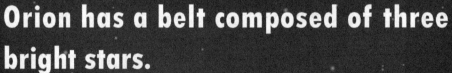 Orion has a belt composed of three bright stars.

ORION

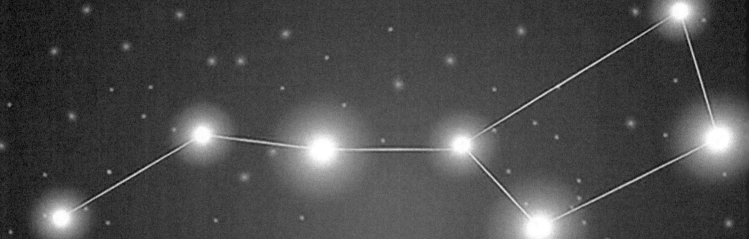

Ursa Maior

This constellation is best seen in April. Its name means "larger bear." It contains the Big Dipper, which is thought of as a constellation, but is actually an asterism.

An asterism is a group of stars that has a name, but is located within a larger constellation. Zeus was attracted to a nymph by the name of Callisto. When his jealous wife Hera found out, she cast a spell and changed Callisto to the form of a bear, and banished her to the skies.

Big Dipper

Ursa Minor

This constellation is best seen in June. Its name means the "smaller bear" and it represents Callisto's son Arcas who was changed into a bear as well. This constellation contains Polaris, which is the North Star. Some people think the North Star should be positioned in a straight line above their heads, but that's only true if you're standing at the North Pole.

Awesome! Now you know more about the constellations in the night sky. You can find more Astronomy and Space books from Baby Professor by searching the website of your favorite book retailer.

Visit

BABY PROFESSOR
EDUCATION KIDS

www.BabyProfessorBooks.com
to download Free Baby Professor eBooks
and view our catalog of new and exciting
Children's Books

9 781541 913936